Hybrid Cars

Karen D. Povey

KIDHAVEN PRESS

An imprint of Thomson Gale, a part of The Thomson Corporation

Detroit • New York • San Francisco • San Diego • New Haven, Conn.
Waterville, Maine • London • Munich

LIBRARY OF CONGRESS CATALOGING-IN-PUBLICATION DATA

Povey, Karen D., 1962-
Hybrid cars / by Karen D. Povey.
p. cm. -- (Our environment)
Includes bibliographical references and index.
ISBN 0-7377-3484-1 (hard cover : alk. paper) 1. Hybrid electric cars—Juvenile literature. I. Title. II. Series.
TL221.15.P68 2006
629.22'93--dc22   2005032334

Printed in China

contents

chapter one

Cars and the Environment

Worldwide, there are over 700 million cars on the road. By 2025, the number of cars will be over a billion. Americans alone drive 235 million cars, traveling over 7 billion miles (11.3 billion km) each day. Most Americans depend on their cars to take them to work or to school. Cars carry people to do their shopping and to visit the doctor. Cars are so essential to the American way of life that most people cannot imagine life without them.

Running on Oil

Moving so many cars over so many miles requires a great deal of fuel. Most car, truck, and bus engines burn gasoline or diesel fuel. These fuels are products made from oil. A lot of oil is used in the United

States. Although the nation is home to only 5 percent of the world's population, it uses 25 percent of the oil produced in the entire world.

People cannot make oil. That means it is a **nonrenewable resource**. Nonrenewable resources, such as oil, coal, and natural gas, were formed over millions of years and cannot be replaced once they are gone.

Oil lies in large pools deep within the Earth, sometimes many miles underground. The amount of oil that exists in the ground is limited and will not last forever. No one knows how much oil is left or when it will be used up.

Rush hour traffic on a Los Angeles freeway gives some idea how essential oil is to the American way of life.

Oil and Pollution

The use of oil has a major impact on the environment. Oil is pumped from the ground and piped or shipped to factories. These factories, called **refineries**, manufacture the oil into products such as gasoline and diesel fuel. Millions of gallons of oil are spilled every year during the pumping or moving of oil to refineries. This spilled oil may harm or kill wildlife and cause damage to sensitive habitats. Refineries create **pollution** as they manufacture gasoline from oil.

However, oil is most harmful to the environment when it is burned as gasoline and diesel fuel in vehicles. When car engines burn gas, they create huge amounts of pollution that affect the quality of air all over the world. Cars produce over 330 million tons (300 million metric tons) of pollution every year in the United States alone. According to the U.S. Environmental Protection Agency, "driving a private car is probably a typical citizen's most 'polluting' daily activity."[1] This pollution can create serious health effects for people.

Smog

When a car burns gasoline, a poisonous mix of chemicals, smoke, soot, and dust emerges from the car's tailpipe. Some of this pollution can be seen in the form of **smog**. Smog is a layer of dirty air that hangs low in the sky over cities. Smog causes breathing problems, such as asthma, and contributes to

A brown cloud hangs over Denver, Colorado, one of many American cities affected by smog.

How Fossil Fuels Contribute to Global Warming

1 All plants take in carbon dioxide from the air.

2 Some prehistoric plants were buried deep in the earth after they died.

3 After millions of years, the dead plants turn into oil and coal, also called fossil fuels.

4 When fossil fuels are burned, they release carbon dioxide and other greenhouse gases into the air.

birth defects. In many large cities around the world, pollution from traffic has made the air quality so bad that people wear masks outside to filter the air they breathe.

However, smog is not limited to large cities. Wind often blows smog away from the places where it was created. Smog drifts over state lines and the borders of countries. Even rural areas can be affected by smog carried on the wind from large, polluted cities hundreds of miles away.

Climate Change

Not all pollution from cars can be seen. One dangerous chemical produced is **carbon monoxide**, an invisible poisonous gas. Carbon monoxide can cause breathing problems and keep a person's brain from functioning properly. Another invisible chemical produced by cars is **carbon dioxide**. For every gallon of gasoline burned in a car's engine, nearly 20 pounds (9kg) of carbon dioxide is released into the environment.

Many scientists believe that the creation of so much carbon dioxide and other gases is causing a gradual increase in the Earth's temperature. The effects of this **global warming** are uncertain. Scientists think it may cause sea levels to rise, change the Earth's weather patterns, and affect the survival of many kinds of plants and animals.

The Clean Air Act

The problems caused by pollution have been known for decades. Scientists and government officials have spent a great deal of time and money to develop solutions to these problems. In 1970 a federal law known as the Clean Air Act was passed to help control pollution from cars and other sources. The law required car manufacturers to develop ways to decrease pollution from the vehicles they made. Car companies responded by creating smog control technology that helped car engines burn gas more cleanly.

Smog and Particles

The Most Polluted U.S. Cities: Smog

1. Los Angeles, CA
2. Visalia–Porterville, CA
3. Bakersfield, CA
4. Fresno, CA
5. Houston, TX
6. Merced, CA
7. Sacramento, CA
8. Hanford, CA
9. Knoxville, TN
10. Dallas–Fort Worth, TX
11. Washington, DC–Baltimore, MD
12. Philadelphia, PA
13. New York, NY
14. Charlotte, NC
15. Cleveland, OH
16. Greensboro, NC
17. Pittsburgh, PA
18. Phoenix, AZ
19. San Diego, CA
20. Modesto, CA

The Most Polluted U.S. Cities: Particles

1. Los Angeles, CA
2. Visalia–Porterville, CA
3. Bakersfield, CA
4. Fresno, CA
5. Pittsburgh, PA
6. Detroit, MI
7. Atlanta, GA
8. Cleveland, OH
9. Hanford, CA
10. Birmingham, AL
11. Cincinnati, OH
12. Knoxville, TN
13. Weirton, WV
14. Chicago, IL
15. Canton, OH
16. Charleston, WV
17. Modesto, CA
18. New York, NY
19. Merced, CA
20. St. Louis, MO

Source: The American Lung Association

The Pollution Problem Remains

Because of changes brought about by the Clean Air Act, each car made today creates 60 to 80 percent less pollution than cars made in the 1960s. As a result, the air in some large cities in the United States has gotten cleaner. However, many cities still have serious problems with pollution.

There are many reasons why pollution is still such a problem. Although cars are getting cleaner, there are more of them. In addition, each car is being driven more miles. Americans now drive four times as many miles each year as they did in

1970. Many people live far from where they work and often do not have access to buses, subways, or trains. Most people drive alone to work, even when vanpools, commuter lanes, and other opportunities for carpooling exist. High-polluting buses and trucks have not been required to reduce pollution as much as cars.

The pollution problem is especially bad in cities in South America, Africa, and Asia. In these regions, there are few laws to control pollution. As cities continue to grow, the problem will only become worse.

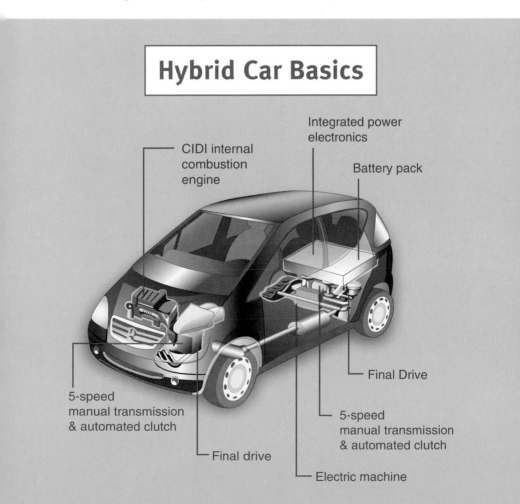

Hybrid Car Basics

CIDI internal combustion engine

Integrated power electronics

Battery pack

5-speed manual transmission & automated clutch

Final drive

Electric machine

5-speed manual transmission & automated clutch

Final Drive

A Pollution Solution?

In response to the growing pollution crisis, in 1990 U.S. government officials created a new version of the Clean Air Act. This law took an even stronger approach to cutting down on pollution. It required oil refineries to change the formula of the gasoline they make so that it will burn cleaner. The law also requires a better system for making sure that pollution-control equipment on cars is working properly.

Faced with requirements to develop cleaner cars and the knowledge that the world's supply of oil is limited, carmakers have been working on developing new technologies for their vehicles. They hope to build cars that use less gas and create less pollution.

The first steps toward fulfilling these goals were taken in 1997, when the first hybrid cars went on sale to the public. Hybrid cars use less gas and run cleaner than other cars. In the coming years, they may play an important role in easing some of the world's environmental problems.

chapter two

The Benefits of Hybrid Cars

One way to conserve oil and create less pollution would be to find ways that cars could drive farther using less gas. The distance that a car can drive with each gallon of gas is known as its **fuel efficiency**. According to the Natural Resources Defense Council, raising the fuel efficiency of cars from the 2005 average of 24 miles per gallon (10km/l) to 40 miles per gallon (17km/l) would cut gasoline use in the United States by one-third and significantly reduce pollution.

Meet the Hybrid

The hybrid car, or hybrid electric vehicle, was developed to meet the goals of high fuel efficiency and low pollution. A hybrid electric vehicle is a

The dashboard display in this hydrogen-electric hybrid car shows the driver the source of the car's power as it is driven.

cross between a gasoline- or diesel-powered car and an electric car. Combining the best features of both types of vehicles allows hybrids to be much more fuel efficient than regular cars.

Like other vehicles, a hybrid car has a gas tank that supplies fuel to an engine that burns gasoline or diesel. But it also has a set of batteries that supply power to an electric motor. Unlike electric cars, a hybrid car never needs to be plugged in. Instead, a generator in the car keeps the batteries charged.

Hybrid Efficiency

Hybrids are more fuel efficient than regular cars for several reasons. In a hybrid, both the gasoline engine and the electric motor can provide power at the same time to move the car. Because it gets help from the electric motor, the gas engine in a hybrid can be much smaller than in regular vehicles. A smaller engine burns less fuel than a larger one.

Another reason a hybrid is fuel efficient is that it does not have to rely on using the gasoline engine all the time. At very low speeds, up to about 15 miles (24km/h) per hour, the hybrid may operate under battery power alone. A hybrid has a complex system of computer controls that help the engine and electric motor work together. When the gasoline engine is not needed, such as at a stoplight, the computer shuts it off completely. By not always having its gasoline engine running, a hybrid saves significantly on fuel.

Because the hybrid's fuel-saving features are automatically controlled by its computer, a driver notices few differences from driving a typical car. At low speeds, when using only electricity, a hybrid is very quiet. At stoplights or in traffic jams, the driver may notice the gasoline engine shutting off. Most hybrids have special displays that the driver can watch to see what type of power is running the car at any given moment.

Saving Fuel

Because of their fuel-saving design, many hybrid electric vehicles can drive twice as far on a gallon of gas as a typical car. The Toyota Prius, for example, averages 45 miles per gallon (19km/l), and the Honda Insight averages 60 miles per gallon (25km/l). Hybrids actually get higher fuel efficiency during city driving than freeway driving, which is the opposite of most vehicles. This happens because the gasoline engine shuts off and the electric motor is used more often in city driving.

Coming Clean

Because they use less gas than other cars, hybrids also create less pollution. For example, a 2005 hybrid Toyota Prius releases 57 percent less carbon monoxide and 90 percent fewer smog-causing chemicals than a nonhybrid 2005 Toyota Camry. James Kliesch of the American Council for an Energy-Efficient Economy points out that "choosing which vehicle to drive is one of, if not *the*, most important environmental decisions a person can make."[2]

Government officials are beginning to recognize the environmental benefit of hybrids. New York City has already begun replacing its dirty diesel buses with diesel-electric hybrids. Officials there also hope to begin replacing the city's fleet of 13,000 taxicabs with hybrids. This move would help clean up the air in one of the most polluted

Since hybrid buses were introduced in Yosemite National Park, emissions there have been reduced by 90 percent.

cities in the United States. In San Francisco, hybrid taxis are already on the street.

Federal officials as well as local ones are increasingly turning to hybrid vehicles. In 2005 the National Park Service replaced eighteen buses in Yosemite National Park with hybrid ones. This has reduced the amount of pollution released by 90 percent. The new buses, with their increased fuel efficiency and quieter ride, are an important step in protecting the fragile Yosemite environment.

Rewards for Going Hybrid

Driving a hybrid not only helps the environment, it may also help the hybrid driver. All over the United States, governments and corporations are offering

incentives, or rewards, to encourage people to drive hybrids. In California, for example, drivers of hybrids that get more than 45 miles per gallon (19 km/l) can use car pool lanes on freeways, even if they are alone in the car. For drivers who deal with California's daily traffic jams, this incentive has been powerful. "Many customers are telling us the carpool lane is the main reason for buying now,"[3] says Dianne Whitmire of Carson Toyota in Southern California.

In California drivers of some hybrid vehicles are allowed to use the carpool lane even when driving alone.

After bypassing traffic in the car pool lane, hybrid drivers may also find that they save money when they pull into a parking spot. From California to Sweden, city governments are rewarding hybrid drivers with reduced-cost or even free parking. In San Jose, California, for example, a hybrid driver displaying a special permit can legally pull up to a parking meter and walk away without paying. Spots in San Jose parking garages are also free to hybrids. Parking costs in that city can reach $300 each month, so this privilege is proving to be a powerful incentive for purchasing a hybrid.

The U.S. government also encourages people to choose hybrids to protect the environment. Depending on which car they buy, people can save up to several thousand dollars on their taxes when they purchase a hybrid. In a speech announcing this tax break, President George W. Bush explained that its goal is to "encourage people to make right choices in the marketplace that will…help improve our environment."[4]

Businesses Go Hybrid

A growing number of companies across the United States are also promoting the purchase and use of hybrid cars. Many of these companies even help their employees purchase hybrid electric vehicles. The leaders of these companies feel that it benefits their companies and communities when their employees drive hybrids.

Leading the way is Hyperion, a computer software company in Santa Clara, California. Hyperion offers employees $5,000 toward the purchase of a hybrid car. Hyperion will provide this incentive to the first 250 employees who purchase a hybrid, at a cost of over 1 million dollars. Hyperion's president, Godfrey Sullivan, says the environmental benefits of the program are worth the cost. "We receive an enormous amount of good will around the globe for this, far beyond the cost of the program. We know we're not necessarily going to change the world through this initiative," he says, "but it's our aim at Hyperion to get people thinking about change, about making a difference."[5] Within the program's first six months, 50 employees purchased hybrids with Hyperion's help.

People are beginning to understand that hybrid electric vehicles are better for the environment than regular cars. But it is unclear if hybrids can solve the long-term problems of the world's dwindling oil supply. Despite their benefits, hybrids have some serious limitations to becoming the solution for the world's future transportation needs.

chapter three

The Limits of Hybrid Cars

Most people choose to buy a hybrid electric vehicle because of its environmental benefits. Many hybrid owners feel that they are taking action to decrease pollution and help the world reduce its use of a nonrenewable energy source. But hybrid cars can only go so far in solving the pollution problems and oil use of cars. Although hybrids use battery power much of the time, they still run on gasoline or diesel fuel. Therefore, as long as hybrids are driven, there will still be a need for oil, and cars will create pollution.

How Much Oil Can Hybrids Save?

Although hybrid cars use less gas than most regular cars, many experts question the true potential that hybrids have for saving large amounts of oil. For example, the 2005 Toyota Prius (the top-selling hybrid) has an average fuel efficiency of about 45

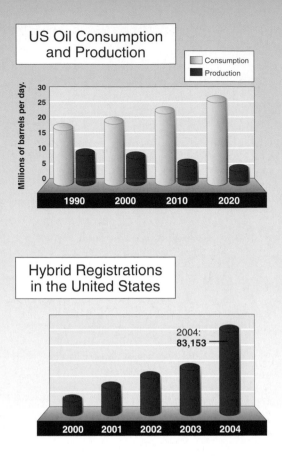

US Oil Consumption and Production

Millions of barrels per day.

Consumption
Production

1990   2000   2010   2020

Hybrid Registrations in the United States

2004: 83,153

2000   2001   2002   2003   2004

miles per gallon (19km/l). A regular car on the road in 2005 had an average fuel efficiency of 21 miles per gallon (9km/l). If both cars were driven 12,000 miles (19,000km) in one year, the Prius would use 267 gallons (1,010l) of gas and the regular car would use 571 gallons (2,161l). Therefore, driving the Prius would save 304 gallons (1,151l) of gas. In 2005 there were about 400,000 hybrids on the road in the United States. With each saving 304 gallons (1,151l) of gas compared to a regular car, the total gas savings is nearly 122 million gallons (462 million l) each year.

Saving this much gas each year might sound like a significant difference. But because there are still so few hybrids on the road compared to regular cars, the overall gas savings barely makes a dent in the amount of oil the United States consumes. The United States uses 390 million gallons (1.5 billion l) of gas every *day*. Even if half of the cars driven in the United States were hybrids, there would still be an enormous demand for the dwindling amounts of oil available for the future.

Experts have difficulty agreeing when world oil supplies will begin to run out. Some believe oil supplies will be able to meet the world's demand until 2030. Many others feel that the amount of oil available will begin to decline within five years. If oil supplies begin dropping within a decade or less, it will be nearly impossible to get the tens of millions of hybrid cars necessary on the road in time to realize large-scale oil savings. Because hybrids are a new technology, automakers need time to design models and gear up factories for making lots of hybrids. And because cars last a long time—fifteen years on average—it will take many years before enough people trade in their old, regular cars for hybrid models. This could be too late for enough oil savings to stretch the remaining supply for any significant amount of time.

A Question of Cost

Even if automobile manufacturers could produce enough hybrid cars quickly, the number of people who buy them will probably remain limited. Most

Many automakers are entering the hybrid car market. This visitor at an auto show in Germany is inspecting a Mercedes hybrid engine.

car buyers do not choose the car they buy based on its effect on the environment. Instead, they look at other features of the car, such as its size, power, comfort, and cost, when making their decisions. Most hybrids do not measure up to regular cars when these other factors are considered.

Hybrids are usually smaller and have less power than regular cars. They also cost several thousand dollars more to buy than similar nonhybrids because of their expensive technology. Some of this additional cost is made up over the life of the car because of money saved at the gas pump. Since a hybrid uses less gas, it costs less to drive. Depending on gas prices, hybrid drivers could save an average of $5,000 in gas costs over the fifteen-year life of the car. However, the money saved on long-term gas expenses barely makes up for the increased up-front cost of a hybrid. Therefore it is likely that only people who can easily afford a higher-priced car will buy a hybrid. The majority of drivers who are less well-off will not be able to afford one.

Most hybrids are sold in developed regions of the world, such as North America, Europe, Australia, and Japan. These regions have environmental protection laws that limit the amount of pollution cars can create. By law, car manufacturers

Owners of hybrid cars save money at the pump because their cars burn less fuel.

in these regions must find ways to increase the fuel efficiency of new models they sell. These laws have been an important factor in encouraging the development and sales of hybrid cars.

However, in many other parts of the world, such as Africa, Asia, and South America, there are fewer laws governing the fuel efficiency and pollution of cars. In these places, automakers can build and sell cars with little regard for the pollution they cause. Because cars without technology to control pollution cost less to build, they are usually much less expensive to buy. Their low price makes these high-polluting cars popular with low-income people in developing countries. Even if they wanted to buy a hybrid, most people in these countries would not be able to afford its much higher price. Unless automakers find ways to reduce costs significantly, it is unlikely that hybrids will ever catch on in these poorer regions of the world, where the number of cars and amount of pollution are increasing rapidly.

Gas-Hungrier Hybrids

One step that automakers are taking to encourage the popularity of hybrids in the United States is to give hybrids the power of regular cars. Original hybrid cars were made with smaller and less powerful gas engines than regular cars. This is one of the reasons they are so fuel efficient. However, the newer hybrids, such as the Honda Accord, Lexus SUV, and Toyota Highlander, have the same size engines as their nonhybrid cousins.

Instead of helping save fuel, the electric motors in these new hybrids give them more power for accelerating quickly. As a result, these new-generation hybrids use nearly as much gas as nonhybrids. For example, the 2005 Honda Accord hybrid saves just 2 miles per gallon (0.7km/l) when compared to the gas-only Accord.

Certain hybrid cars with larger gas engines, such as this 2005 Honda Accord, consume nearly as much fuel as a gas-only version.

This new use of hybrid technology concerns some conservationists who feel that it defeats the whole purpose of a hybrid's value in saving gas and decreasing pollution. Others, however, feel that making hybrids more like regular cars will help them catch on more quickly. Jon Coifman, spokesperson for the National Resources Defense Council, says, "In the grand scheme it's going to be important that drivers don't automatically associate hybrids with sacrifice."[6] Coifman feels that buying a hybrid with slightly better gas mileage is still better than not buying a hybrid at all.

Too Little Too Late?

Regardless of how many people become hybrid owners in the decades to come, the change to hybrid technology may be too late. No matter how fuel efficient cars become, there will come a time in the future that the fuel needed to run gas-powered cars will run out. For this reason, some automakers and research scientists think it is wasteful to put so much time and money into developing hybrids. Many other companies, however, are making large investments of time and money in hybrid technology. These companies think hybrids will play a large role in the future of transportation.

chapter Four

The Future of Hybrid Cars

Each year, car buyers are increasingly choosing hybrids. Since the introduction of the Honda Insight into the United States in 1999, hybrid sales have doubled every year. Nine hybrid models, manufactured by Honda, Toyota, Ford, Chevrolet, General Motors, and Lexus, were sold in the United States in 2005. When they first came out, many of these cars were so popular that people had to wait weeks or months for one to become available to purchase.

Soon hybrid buyers will have more choices. Experts predict as many as 38 hybrid vehicles will be in dealerships by 2011. These new models will include pickup trucks, sports utility vehicles, even sports cars—all powered by hybrid technology.

Much of the hybrid's growing popularity has been driven by increasing gas prices. In April 2005, a survey of people shopping for cars showed that nearly half of them considered the price of gas when deciding on what model of car to buy. Bradley Berman, editor of Hybridcars.com, welcomes this new attitude. "All we've been hearing for 15 years is that consumers don't care about fuel efficiency, that they care more about cupholders than fuel economy," he says. "I would say that fuel economy is the new cupholder."[7]

Debating the Hybrid's Future

Despite their increasing availability and popularity, hybrids still represent a very small number of vehicles on the road, making up only 1.3 percent of U.S. car and truck sales in 2005. Some experts predict that this will always be the case. They argue that because hybrids are more expensive than nonhybrids, they will never have mass appeal. If their predictions are correct, hybrids will account for only about 3 percent of vehicles by 2010.

Other experts see a different future for hybrids. The U.S. Department of Energy estimates that hybrids will make up 10 to 15 percent of new car sales by 2012. Another company that studies the sales of hybrids, Booz Allen Hamilton, says the actual number could be even higher. Experts there predict hybrids will make up 20 percent of new car sales by 2010 and as much as 80 percent by 2015.

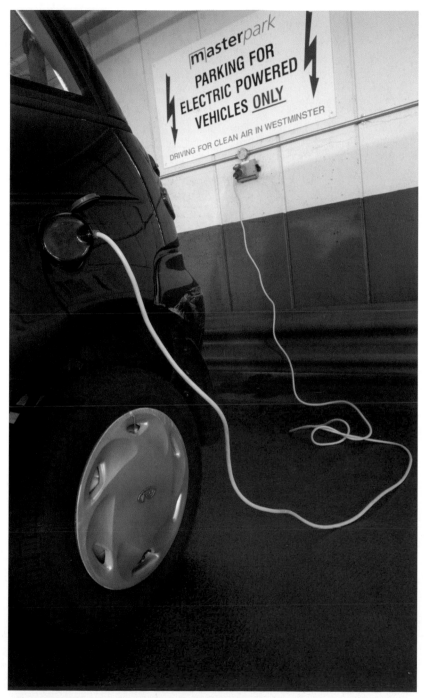

An electric car charges up. Some newer hybrid cars can be charged by plugging them into an electrical outlet.

If that many hybrids are sold, it will have a pay-off for the environment by reducing pollution and improving air quality. But today's hybrids are only a temporary solution to the problem of declining oil supplies. Even if all cars were hybrids, they would still need to run on gas. Because gas is made from a decreasing supply of oil, it will run out some day.

Hybrid Plug-Ins

Some researchers are trying to address this problem by changing hybrid cars to make them less

Japan's prime minister test-drives an experimental car powered by a lithium-ion battery.

dependent on gas. These modified cars are called plug-in electric hybrid vehicles. Plug-ins have far greater fuel efficiency than regular hybrids—from 80 to 230 miles per gallon (28–81km/l).

The key to a plug-in's efficiency lies in greatly increasing its use of electricity. To create a plug-in, the hybrid's original batteries are replaced with much more powerful ones, called lithium-ion batteries. The driver plugs a cord from the car into an electric outlet in the garage to recharge the batteries overnight. The electricity from the batteries is enough to cover the power needs for most short trips the driver takes in a day, usually about 20 to 30 miles (32–48km). When the battery charge runs low, the car switches to using its gas engine, just like a regular hybrid.

This results in huge gas and money savings for plug-in drivers. Even though they must pay for the electricity used to charge the batteries overnight, this cost is significantly less than that of gasoline. For example, driving a standard car 25 miles (40km) costs between $2 and $3 in fuel. A plug-in driven the same distance would cost only 30 cents in electricity and use no gas at all.

The other advantage of plug-ins is that because they use so little gas, they create very little pollution. In fact, when running on electricity alone, plug-ins create no pollution at all. And although the power plant that makes the electricity used to charge the batteries does pollute, this amount of pollution is less than that created by burning gasoline. Overall, plug-ins create two-thirds less pollution than regular cars.

The Downside of Plug-Ins

Even though plug-ins show a great deal of promise, car manufacturers have been slow to accept the idea. For that reason, most plug-ins are created by independent researchers, often tinkering on their cars in their garages. Major car companies are concerned by the high cost of the lithium battery pack. The conversion of a hybrid to a plug-in adds $6,000 to $12,000 to the cost of the car. That is quite a bit more than most car buyers would be willing to pay.

Fans of plug-ins urge both the government and car manufacturers to invest the time and money into developing less expensive lithium batteries. With more research, they expect this could happen in three to five years. For the time being, however, only one car company, DaimlerChrysler, has committed to making some plug-ins available to buyers.

Looking Beyond Hybrids

Some automakers, especially the Japanese companies Toyota and Honda, have invested heavily in hybrids. Many American automakers, on the other hand, have spent more of their research efforts on other technologies. General Motors, for example, has concentrated on developing other types of

This is a model of a hydrogen fuel cell, which uses hydrogen, oxygen, and water to produce electricity.

Plant-based fuels, such as ethanol, may reduce the consumption of oil.

vehicle fuels. Officials at this company feel that moving away from oil-based fuels completely is the only real way to cut back on the use of oil and reduce pollution. Researchers at other companies, however, believe that hybrids are a vital first step in developing other ways of moving vehicles. They hope to apply what they have learned so far to develop future generations of cars that use even less oil and create even less pollution.

Most car manufacturers are also studying new solutions that would make cars completely gas free. These ideas include finding new sources of fuel, such as corn and other plant products. In addition, car companies have already invested many millions of dollars in developing clean-burning fuel cells that run on hydrogen. Most experts agree that the future of cars holds many possibilities. "The auto industry has had variations of the gasoline engine but it has never really seen a situation like this, where you have many very different technologies, each offering promise and vying to become the engine of the future,"[8] says Dan Kahn of Edmunds.com, a car-shopping Web site.

Will hybrids become the car of the future? Or will hybrids serve as a link to even newer and better technologies? At stake is the much-needed solution for the environmental problems caused by today's car culture.

Notes

Chapter 1: Cars and the Environment

1. Environmental Protection Agency, *Automobile Emissions: An Overview*, EPA Office of Mobile Sources Fact Sheet OMS-5, August 1994, p. 6.

Chapter 2: The Benefits of Hybrid Cars

2. Quoted in John Rockhold, "Green Means Go," *Mother Earth News*, October/November 2005, p. 28.
3. Quoted in John O'Dell, "Prices Soar for Hybrids with Rights to Fast Lane," *Los Angeles Times*, August 27, 2005, p. C1.
4. Quoted in Matthew L. Wald, "Designed to Save, Hybrids Burn Gas in Drive for Power," *New York Times*, July 17, 2005, p. 1.16.
5. Quoted in Hybridcars.com, "Private Incentives." www.hybridcars.com/private incentives.

Chapter 3: The Limits of Hybrid Cars

6. Quoted in Brian Handwerk, "Hybrid Cars Losing Efficiency, Adding Oomph," *National Geographic News*, August 8, 2005,

http://news.nationalgeographic.com/news/2005/
08/0808_050808_hybrid_cars.html.

Chapter 4: The Future of Hybrid Cars

7. Quoted in Mark Clayton, "Can Hybrids Save
   US from Foreign Oil?" *Christian Science Monitor*,
   May 19, 2005, p. 14.
8. Quoted in Neal E. Boudette, "Out of Gas: A
   Look at the Current State—and Future
   Potential—of Alternative-Fuel Technologies,"
   Wall Street Journal, July 25, 2005, Eastern edi-
   tion, p. R6.

Glossary

carbon dioxide: A gas formed by the burning of gasoline in car engines.

carbon monoxide: A highly poisonous gas formed by the burning of gasoline in car engines.

fuel efficiency: The distance a car can drive with each gallon of gasoline.

global warming: An increase in the average temperature of the Earth's atmosphere.

incentives: Rewards given to encourage people to behave in a certain way.

nonrenewable resource: A natural resource from the Earth that is in limited supply and cannot be replaced when it is used up.

pollution: Contamination of the natural environment as a result of human activities.

refineries: Factories where oil is manufactured into gasoline.

smog: Visible air pollution caused by a reaction between sunlight and the chemicals released when cars burn fuel.

For Further Exploration

Books

Kris Hirschmann, *Our Environment: Pollution.* San Diego, CA: KidHaven, 2004. The author examines the steps taken to decrease pollution caused by cars and other sources.

Kimberly M. Miller, *What if We Run Out of Fossil Fuels?* Danbury, CT: Children's Press, 2002. This book examines what life would be like without cars or other modern machines fueled by oil. The author also looks at alternative energy sources to prepare for a future without fossil fuels.

Simon Scoones, *Climate Change: Our Impact on the Planet.* New York: Raintree Steck-Vaughn, 2002. An in-depth look at the Earth's changing climate presented with both facts and different expert points of view.

Alvin Silverstein, Virginia Silverstein, and Laura Silverstein Nunn, *Global Warming.* Brookfield, CT: Twenty-first Century, 2003. The book looks at the causes and effects of global warming. The authors also present research into alternative energy sources as a way to stop global warming.

Web Sites

How Stuff Works
(www.auto.howstuffworks.com/hybrid-car. htm). This site contains detailed information on how hybrid cars work. It explains the hybrid's technology in clear detail, including helpful, animated three-dimensional graphics.

HybridCars.com (www.hybridcars.com). This site contains a great deal of information on all things related to hybrid cars. It also compares the environmental impact of hybrid electric cars to regular cars.

Union of Concerned Scientists
(www.ucsusa.org/clean_vehicles/vehicles_health/ cars-and-trucks-and-global-warming). This site contains a great deal of information on the environmental impacts of driving, including global warming and human health.

United States Environmental Protection Agency
(www.epa.gov/otaq/invntory/overview/ pollutants/index). This government site provides detailed information on the different types of pollution caused by cars, including gases such as carbon monoxide and carbon dioxide.

Index

Picture credits

Cover © Jim Sugar/CORBIS

Maury Asseng, 11

AP/Wide World Photo, 14, 18, 35, 36

© David Cooper/Toronto Star/ZUMA/CORBIS, 27

© Salem Krieger/ZUMA/CORBIS, 25

© Alexander Ruesche/CORBIS, 24

© Ted Spiegel/CORBIS, 7

© Bill Varie/CORBIS, 5

Al Golub/UPI/Landov, 17

Bloomberg News/Landov, 35

EPA/Landov, 32

Steve Zmina, 22 (both)

About the Author

Karen D. Povey has spent her career as a conservation educator, working to instill an appreciation for wildlife and wild places in people of all ages. Karen makes her home in Tacoma, Washington, where she presents live animal education programs at Point Defiance Zoo & Aquarium. She has written many books on wildlife and the environment, including *Leopards, Owls, The Condor*, and *Life in a Swamp*. Karen drives a hybrid Toyota Prius as part of her commitment to living green.